FACE OF LEADERSHIP

By

EDERSON LAMBERT

"Personal Leadership of the face in the Mirror "

I dedicate this book to my former fellow Military Instructors at NTTC Meridian Mississippi, the place where I learned the truest value of Leadership.

Table of Contents

Chapter 1 - Leaders Are Ready to Lead.................... pg. 09

1. Face in The Mirror
2. Leadership State of Mind
3. Legendary Military Knife hand
4. Leaders Remember the ALWAYS
5. The BE Simplicities

Chapter 2 - Leaders Take Action...............................pg. 47

6. Wake Up Early
7. Groom Yourself
8. Dress Well
9. Smell Good
10. Good Body Posture

Chapter 3 - Leaders Make Plans................................. pg. 57

11. Make Plans
12. Short Term Plans
13. Long Term Plans
14. POAM
15. Learn Your Environment
16. Always do Research
17. Ask Questions
18. Listen to People
19. Respond Politely
20. Speak Clearly

21. Positive Optimism
22. Follow Your Values
23. Self-Control

Chapter 4 - Leaders Execute Plans................... pg. 79

24. Always follow Through
25. Leaders Remember the ALWAYS
26. The BE Simplicities
27. Simplicity vs Complexity
28. Strive For Balance
29. Life Long Leadership

Leaders Are Ready to Lead!

Leadership should not scare you, rather it should embolden you and it should endow you with confidence to be the kind of leader others willingly follow by being brilliant on the simplicities of self-leadership.

– Ederson Lambert

Face in the Mirror:

The idea of leadership sounds so novel, like some great force that molds and shapes the world unafraid, passionately, fiercely with great elucidation, almost as if it is instinctive. People who lead do so effortlessly as if some were born with it. No one ever really questions ones' leaders because they simply know what's best right? Leaders simply know where to take us, as if they know precisely where all of us are going and therefore we follow without question. But what if I told you that leadership is not just something for people in positions of power. What if I told you that leadership is a clear, transparent and novel concept that belongs to all of us and that it is not instinctive but cultivated? Leaders who lead effortlessly have to train and build their selves up to that point. That leadership is an internal concept that exists within the mind and is supposed to be utilized for your betterment. That leadership is a tool, an auspicious idea that can be honed and fashioned for your benefit. Leadership belongs to us all. It belongs to you, it belongs to me and everyone else in this world who chooses to adopt its values for positive use. It is both the responsibility and delight of those willing to see beyond the reclusive selfishness of doubt within, beyond the burden of personal incurrence which hinders successful use of the concept in order to prosecute an objective. If you can master the subtle nuisance, the gentle balance of positive self-ism and optimistic regard for others for greater good, for personnel and professional growth, to benefit and enhance the well-being of others in a community, than you have what it takes to be a leader. Good positive leadership should not scare you, rather it should embolden you and it should endow you with confidence to be the kind of leader others willingly follow by being both familiar and brilliant on the simplicities as well as being intuitively astute to the complexities of leadership – even more importantly self-leadership. You should be a leader who is resourceful, resilient and compassionate all the same. Moreover assuming the mantle of leadership of self; for the person that is within, mastering leadership of the individual in the mirror, allows one to confidently assume the leadership responsibility of others when needed most. You ever wonder why you never stop to ask yourself, am I a leader? Am I good enough to lead and make such impact? It's true because many of us are so busy that we forget in the bustle of our day to day to even stop and wonder that. Whether you know you are a leader or not. You probably don't even think about it. But what if it were true. What if you were, what if you could. You can imagine that every day you wake up, you stand in front of the mirror in your home, you look at your face and you walk away without ever talking to or telling yourself, I am a leader. It is quite possible you have never bothered at all to operationally pause and address the potential magnate within you. You walk and stand in front of that mirror, you brush your teeth, you wash your face, you comb your hair or cut your hair, shave your face and wash your face again and you leave – or rather you don't shave and you don't cut your hair, you probably brush your teeth, do your hair, put it up, put on some make up, some light lip gloss and walk away because you are not about wearing all that lipstick – or maybe you are, but either way, you always walk away afterwards without that conversation. In all the time you perform all those routine tasks, you have never once taken the time to look at you, the leader, and the person in the mirror and address that potential. You and the leader within never get the chance to interact with each other. You are always too busy passing each other by. Do you not ever wonder how come? Maybe you know – I'm already a leader! Maybe you are asking - Am I already a leader? Perhaps you are – perhaps you are not, or maybe you are unsure. Maybe you just need to pause and look within and reaffirm, maybe to sharpen that inner leadership a little bit, maybe you need to do so a lot, maybe you don't need to polish at all because you are already there, but rather you just need a tool to help you bring up some potential leaders around you. This may be the perfect time to pause one moment in front of that mirror and ask the questions. Is my leadership good enough? Is the leadership around me good enough? Am I being led by good leaders? This honestly may not be a complete tool bag with all your answer, but this may be one of many potential tools that can help you and others hone your skills on this leadership journey.

Every one of us at one point or another in our lives will be challenged with a leadership role or dilemma – whether we want it or not. Maybe you'll become a parent, a boss, a coach, a volunteer activist, a politician, a service member, a police officer, an older sibling – you never know. An at that point in life when you reach the moment of leadership role or dilemma, you are going to have to step to the plate. How you react to those challenges is what will determine the type of leader you rise in the occasion to become. Leadership is the responsibility and delight of those willing to see beyond the seldom recognizable, reclusive selfishness within, beyond the burden of incurrence. Moreover assuming the mantle of leadership for self-determination and self-conduct; for the person that is within determines the kind of leadership we are remembered for. Mastering leadership of the individual in the mirror, allows one to confidently assume the leadership responsibility of others. The reality of truth is that you cannot lead without recognizing your own authority to lead yourself. There is a confidence required to achieve such a feat for yourself. When you do not recognize yourself in the mirror as a person capable of leading the individual that represents you, it is hard to answer the very real question of how do I lead others to achievement? And if I cannot lead myself, the possibility of leading others is not realistic. Not impossible, but likely improbable without self-recognition, self-correction change and application. In the moment there can be many reasons you can fault, point to and see the things that makes you unworthy of being a leader. But that is not what this book is intended to do. It is not intended to condemn you or your leadership journey – rather it is intended to assist you and enhance your potential leadership skill.

Leadership State of Mind:

I can tell you without a doubt that leadership is a state of mind. The measurement of your leadership ability is not necessarily a sum of your past faults or failures, matter of fact any bumps and hiccups you've experienced should serve to enhance and hone your journey. Leadership is an understanding of your personal abilities to positively administer circumstance. And even though you can compromise with your ability to lead in a moment in time, when it seems unrealistic due to circumstance, I will tell you that leading is not an impossibility. It is achievable and practical like any skill to be learned and honed. I get questions all the time from many of my peers, and from young people in my line of work, in the military, in the corporate community, on travel and places volunteering and many others I encounter all over the world where I've ventured – they all ask – how can leadership play a role in my life? And in each instance they are absolutely curious about my role as a leader and how balancing leadership has worked so well for me in my position. These people are always asking me about the term leadership and how the term applies in what I do. They ask me questions like, what is leadership to you Chief. Why do we need it? Why is it important and how do I go about getting some of it? How do I acquire the art of leadership? Who can teach me to be a leader, especially when some leaders can be so disconnected? How do I become a better leader?

I want to first start out by stating all the things that leadership is not. I can tell you for a fact, that leadership is not a drink; it is not a beverage, it is not like a cup of coffee at Starbucks to be bought and sipped before a morning meeting to pump you up and get you ready to go and take over the world. I wish it were. Leadership is not a coat, for you to throw on and take off and thrown in the closet when you are done using it at the end of the day. Leadership is not a part time job to be worked between certain hours of the day and then clock out of it with smiles of freedom. Leadership is not lunch in a drive through. And sadly leadership is not something that can be taught to you at some symposium by some great and mighty orator in one day or even a week.

Leadership is something more. Leadership is a lifetime commitment to yourself. Leadership is a commitment to others who commit to follow you. Leadership starts at home with you. It's something that comes from within and believe it or not is found inside all of us. Not just those who are successful, famous or in high positions. Leadership is defined in many terms, many ways, and at times depending on who is defining it can even have many meanings. I will tell you that Leadership is an experience. Leadership is a state of mind. It is for certain that leadership can be defined as the art of making people feel safe and comfortable around you. It is a state of mind where people are adequately at ease and open minded enough in your presence to listen to your ideas and reciprocate by sharing theirs. Leadership is a conversation of self and at times an understanding between two or more people. All leaders lead by following. One can only lead by learning to follow. Following the basics and becoming brilliant about those basics. Leaders follow to learn, to understand and lead because they understand.

My name is Ederson Lambert; I am a Veteran of the United States Navy. I have been leading people for over 20 years and I can tell you as a leader, I have also had to follow.

Because a true leader follows the basics, is brilliant and masterful about following the path of success. In my 20 years, I have been around many kinds of leaders. Many people who I have learned a great deal from about leadership and more. One of the things I learned is that every one of those people I encountered all had their own leadership styles. These many leaders fit in many categories; Some were Inspiring leaders, some were charismatic leaders, motivating leaders, experienced leaders, ambitious leaders, friendly leaders, loving leaders, motherly leaders, big ones, little ones, tall leaders, short leaders, happy leaders, angry leaders, good ones as well as bad ones and somehow someway all those people have been leaders in their own rights. They all impacted me with their leadership. What I remember most importantly about them was that people chose to follow them all. For some it was the kind of leader they needed or had wanted and for others it was simply because it was convenient. I don't consider myself to be a leader that the world would call on to lead the free nations, but I can say that based on my experience in my career that I have been called a leader many times. As far as leadership qualifications go, for good and for bad, people have looked upon me at one point or another as someone whose ideas have been worth listening to and that I have been worth sharing an idea or two with. And I stand humbled because of that. People trusted me enough to honor me with that title. I thought it only fitting that I share my short take on the meaning and expectations of being a leader.

The truth is leadership is a word that describes a person and also describes many a great people, however the word itself should not be used only and simply to describe great persons, but should describe all people. It can be used to describe you for instance. You can say, well I'm not a leader. I don't lead a great group of people. I don't command or tell anyone what to do. I say that anyone can be a leader and I mean it when I say that you are a leader because leaders don't always have to be great in order to lead. A lot of times it is normal and ordinary people like you and I that become great leaders by virtue of doing simple acts that people later quantify as great. You are a leader the moment you were born. You've been leading your whole life. It only takes a simple act to make you great. And that simple act is not something you go out of your way to do because you know that it will automatically be great, but it is a simple characterization of your deeds and integrity that someone else will interpret as a great act and they in term will probably label you a great leader for that simple act. Jesus Christ in the bible characterizes the idea of leadership as a concept of service and sacrifice to others, and is not simply the act of lording and ruling over people. It is serving other people.

I say to you, that you are a leader right now. I can tell you that you are a leader right in this very moment. And I'll prove it to you. When you wake up in the morning and walk to the bathroom and look at the mirror, you are looking at a leader. That face reflecting back at you, is the true Face of Leadership.
When you wake up in the morning every day and you look at yourself in the mirror, if you don't say to yourself that you are looking at a leader than you are not being truthful to whom you

are. If you are a woman you are a leader. If you are a man you are a leader. If you are a husband, if you are a wife you are a leader. If you are a father, a mother, grandmother or a grandfather than you are a leader. If you have a job or a career you are a leader. The simple fact is that every day that you wake up and walk out of your house and see someone and greet them, believe it or not you are committing an act of leadership and that makes you are a leader. That gesture of you being near and close enough to see someone and interact with them makes you a leader. You would not believe how the simplicity of that act; how the simplicity of your leadership starts. It starts in baby steps. It starts very simply by looking at, smiling and acknowledging other people. It starts by greeting one another politely. It starts when you see that very first person and they look at you and they say good morning. After saying good morning, they look at you and their eyes light up. They tilt their head up acknowledging you and are waiting for you to say something to them in return. That is an act of leadership right there. The reality is that you have been learning all your life to be a leader. You have had examples of leadership in your life teaching you since you were a child. Think about it:

you have been learning to lead from your mother, from your father, your grandparents, your older siblings, from your teachers, policemen, firefighters, doctors and all the people you have come in contact with who have played positional authorities in your life. And low and behold you have now become those very people and or you are on your way to taking over some of those roles. From being a parent to a career field that puts you dead center in a leadership role. So no, there is no running from leadership in your life. How you embrace and administer that leadership is what defines you as a leader.

The very first intention that occurred is the fact the person chose to look at you.

That intention is a very subliminal request for leadership. It doesn't mean the person needs your leadership; it simply is the way the nature of leadership works. People don't need you to tell them what to do, or want necessarily to be told anything, but it is a social condition that exists among people that requires us to look for ques of safety and direction around us as we travel on our day to day. This unassuming mindset is why people greet each other, and what people have become accustomed to which allows us to look for queues in other people. I call it leadership. It can also simply be referred to as guidance, or directional markers. Those social queues are cues of acceptance, of safety and clear direction. We look up to the stars at night for guidance. We look up at signs on the road when we are driving. We look up for leadership. We look for the sun in the daytime to know where and when we are. Simply put, life would be somewhat difficult without direction and safety markers.

So the look towards you is a very quiet and subtle supplication for a visual response from you a stranger or someone they may or not know, simply to tell them firstly that you are okay. To tell them that you are safe to be around and that you could even be helpful and beneficial to them. That is why people choose to be led. It is not for any other reason but for their well-being, safety and benefit. Simple basic needs. That is why we choose to lead or be led by other people at work, in our careers, at church, in politics, in the military and etc. Your cue to respond in the morning to someone looking at you is naturally to respond with positive mannerisms, a good morning and a disarming smile. You have just led that person to believe that you are safe and are okay to be around or to be near.

Some people think that because they weren't born as Alpha males and females, role leading driven characters who are loud, vocal and charismatic that somehow they aren't leadership material. Some believe that their inexperience makes them less of a leader then others. That could not be farther from the truth. The person that you probably ignore the most in life when it comes to leading is yourself. And there is no better place to start. Most of us don't see ourselves as leaders or as someone who has good direction in life because we have been comfortable with being led. We look at the mirror and we see ourselves and think well we must not cut it. We don't look like the president of the United States; we don't look like the Senators and Congresswomen and men and the fancy generals in the military or the admirals on the fancy Navy ships. We must not be leadership material. But I tell you that you could not be farther from that idea. President Donald Trump became president not because of his years of great experience in politics, but because he believes in himself as a leader. President Obama and President Bush, President Vladimir Putin of Russia all have the same characteristics as leaders – they all simply are confident in themselves and perceptive enough to have recognized, honed the talents within and their leadership drive allowed them to ascend to a place of community leadership. You may not aspire to become a president or General and that is okay too. You may simply want to inspire yourself with confidence to excel on your day to day career. You are the exact leadership that you need to be to get your life in the right direction today. Not like anyone else who the world has dubbed a great and charismatic leader. Those persons and others who I have mentioned may be an inspiration to strive for, but it by no means takes anything away from your own abilities to lead the person staring at you in the mirror when you wake up in the morning.

Leadership is you and your ideas and how far you want them to reach. Leaders present their ideas to people who want to listen, they present their thoughts to people who are receptive and are willing to help them build it. People who listen to these leaders are persons who feel safe around that leader, people who feel that person cares enough about them to acknowledge them. People who feel they can get good directions from a leader will sit and listen to their ideas all day. That is the leadership trait that we must all learn to cultivate in order to have people be receptive and understanding of our points of view.

The first and most important thing about being a leader is to always be willing to serve. Being humble enough to listen and to follow. Good leaders are always willing to listen and do so carefully. Good leaders are followers and what I mean by that is good leaders are humble enough to recognize that they are not jack of all trades that they too have knowledge shortfalls and therefore good leaders should follow good advice. Therefore good leaders are followers. It is said that all great leaders were themselves once followers, but I will take it a step further and tell you that leaders are still followers because they will always need knowledgeable people around them to lead and assist them in making well and informed decisions. Meaning that if you are the leader of the person in the mirror, you have to be willing to do two important things; you have to know how to follow and you have to be willing to take direction yourself. It's not always about telling others what to do. It is always more about listening. **LISTEN MORE.** Talk less. And when you speak, let it be the sharing of good ideas to make those who choose to follow you feel safe, so that they know they too have a voice with you. Let it be the sharing and giving of good direction. Let your words be of good intentions of benefit to them. Good intentions will always get others to listen.

It starts with you leader. It always starts with you. Your good intentions always begin and end in your mind. Your self-leadership will reflect outwardly when you have mastered the good intentions of your heart and your mind to lead yourself in better and safer directions in life. First you have to lead yourself by giving yourself the proper direction that you need. You do so by being vocal and expressing the ideas you have about leading your life in the right direction, it is then you will have taken the first steps. It sounds like a cliché but the direction of your life always starts within yourself and never without yourself. It is a discipline that must be hone – leadership of self. Equanimity is a goal for all good leaders. The leadership that you project is reflective of your inner order and still waters. Still waters run deep and people are more apt to drink the cool aid when you know the root of the source. People will receive your good intentions when they know and understand how deep and calm the source goes. They will always respect and listen when you give them kindness, sweetness and depth and nothing else. People who follow you will trust and believe you when you give them peace of mind instead of displacement or chaos.

The second step is following your precepts, the simplicities that keeps you disciplined, the very ideas that you have set out for yourself which sets you apart as a leader. Follow your discipline faithfully so that you accomplish them with purpose and intent. Self-Inhibitions, self-doubt, fear, uneasiness, fear of failure and lack of knowledge are some of the many obstacles of leadership that hinders your discipline. But do not be fooled by the complexities that barricades your path. They are necessary to help you grow, but make no mistake you must absolutely prosecute and subdue them. Those minor hurdles are what keep us from staring directly into the eyes of the face in the mirror. The hardest part of leadership is living a double standard; asking things of people that you aren't willing to do yourself. Asking people to share what you aren't willing to share. To give up things, you yourself aren't willing to give up, asking of people to share their ideas when you yourself will not share in return. It is the hardest thing that keeps many of us stagnant as leaders. That is the very thing that is not allowing you, the person to accomplish the task of being a leader. You and only you can convince yourself that you have what it takes to lead yourself out and through any complex situation that you encounter in this life. It is simply selfishness that must be subjugated. You must overcome the fear and idleness of personal hindrances in your mirror. When that person walking towards you in the hallway or on the street sees you in the morning and greet you, instead of responding, you look away or turn away from them and keep on walking without a positive response back, you have just given away an opportunity to lead. Firstly that is the rudest thing you can do to another person in the street or a hallway. When they go out of their way to acknowledge you and you pretend that you didn't even hear them. That is the worst thing that you can do as a leader to people who look up to you for leadership, by not acknowledging them you give up your credibility.

You must always remember that you represent you in all aspects of what you do. In all aspects of what must be accomplished to reach any and all goals set before you. You are the face of your leadership. For better or for worse you have to be true to yourself and you have to be sincere in leading yourself, which in retrospect will give credence to you in leading others. Otherwise they will see it for what it is and will stop listening to your ideas.

A leader must always be willing to serve. A good leader must be humble. A good leader does not allow their ego to lead. A hubris leader will drive away good ideas and good intentions because of their lack of judgement. In the end a good leader should always be willing to listen. **Listen more.** Listen more and only give your good ideas – only, when the person has stopped speaking and begins to wait for your safe leadership directions. Always listen more.

Legendary Knife Hand:

Leadership is not just about leading others. It is about leading yourself in the manner that will allow others to follow you. These are some of the most essential and basic rules that I learned as a leader in the service. First I will say that the legendary military knife and the concept of what is being implied of it, in this conversation is only being brought up as a metaphor for leadership direction. The knife hand in itself is a real gesture utilize to point at someone or something to gain maximum attention. It is effective as it is poignant. I first became acquainted with the legendary knife hand in a time in my life, when I was in need of much direction and at a point in which I had little confidence in my leadership abilities. I first learned about the knife hand in boot camp as a young sailor in Great Lakes, IL in the summer of 2000 where my Recruit Division Commanders would use it to point and speak to me about matters that I needed to understand as a service member. He used it at great lengths to get my attention, to get a tasker and many a goals accomplished.

I have always been fond of the martial gesture since and have incorporate it in my life as a subliminal and metaphorical tool for good leadership direction. In my teaching tenure as a military Instructor in Mississippi, I used the same concept to motivate and instruct my students in completing and effectively getting goals done. It wasn't the gesture alone that made the point, but it was the idea, the discipline and concept of it and the potency of its meaning which made it effective.

The history of the knife hand can be traced going back many decades within the military ranks as a way to garner the immediate attention of someone you are leading for a very specific reason. The practice or term knife hand goes back hundreds of years in the form of hand to hand combat and possibly even earlier in the Martials arts world in Asia. The suggestive military knife hand is used in the same manner, but not in the combative sense today. It is used to simply represent or point to a sense of order and discipline to achieve a goal or complete a mission. The famous gesture is even made famous in the movie Spartacus where the slave general is on the battlefield and preparing to march against the Roman Army and he then directs his troops to march forward in order to accomplish the task of fighting the Romans. In that setting it is used as a leadership tool and that is how and why I am referencing it in this manual.

Over many years the gesture though still widely used in the military has become for me in the civilian environment as a metaphorical tool. It is spoken in many conversations I have and I have introduced the concept to personnel who have never heard of the term before to their appreciation and adoptive satisfaction. The gesture has been used by countless leaders as a visual tool to point forward and delineates some very basic, disciplined and effective advice or objective for living life. Some of these advices can range from as simple as putting your pants on one leg at a time, to tying your shoes in a way that allows all your laces to look aligned. It can help motive you to adopt certain behaviors in life, behaviors that can lead to real and positive change if they are practiced and adhered to. And if you are faithful enough in practicing those simple behaviors they can allow you to reach a level of success. In this short pamphlet I have listed a few essential things to help you get you through your day. I have listed some daily routines to remind you that you are the driver in the seat of the car that is your life. And that it is okay to drive yourself safely on the road by ensuring that you have a map and a plan to get where you need to go. All leaders need basic instruction and direction. It starts by preparing yourself as a leader.

There is no trick to this leadership think. There is no complicated explanation to what you are supposed to do or be as a leader. The basic truth about leadership is when you look at yourself in the mirror and point to yourself you recognize immediately who you are. You know exactly what your weaknesses are and what your strengths are. You know deep down that you are your own adversary, you are your own fiercest enemy and that you and only you can overcome your fears and doubts by overcoming life's complexities with the remedy of self-discipline and by being brilliant and knowledgeable on the simplicities of leadership. When you look into the mirror and point, you must be determined in your heart to conquer your shortcomings, conquer your inhibitions by simply being true to you and by being familiar about the simplicities. The knife hand is not meant to be used in a literal sense, it never was. It's a metaphor for leadership, for self-control, for harnessing and honing your purpose in a positive direction. One does not simply wake up and go straight to work. It takes effort, it takes preparation and you have to start by giving yourself the opportunity to go in the right direction. It starts with pointing to the way you want to go. So yes, point your arm and your palms toward your goal in the mirror and follow through.

Leaders are constantly learning. We are students of disciplines I call simplicities. We subordinate complexities and make them easy for others to follow. Leader are confident, assertive and nonaggressive. You have to learn to present yourself in a nonthreatening manner. You also have to learn to execute without hesitation an art that is found in the balance between fierceness and subtlety. In the end decisiveness shows confidence and expertise. You must be balanced both mentally and physically. You must love yourself, to appreciate yourself, by complimenting and telling yourself that you can, you will, you must and nothing will stop you from overcoming. That is the power of self-leadership, self-start, self-will, the power of self-control, self-confidence. And that is the greatest personal achievement that you can attain. Master yourself and simply be who you are. Point and go where you need it like a missile. Fire and forget-not. Be decisive in your expertise and throughput.

Some of the terms accompanied with self in the first half of those compound words literally refers to using your own energy and determination to make things happen. As leaders a lot of times we have people that work for us and help us to execute our visions, but I can tell you that personal leadership of self means you have to apply and achieve your goals on your own, not necessarily by yourself, but it does mean you have to reach a point of confidence high enough that you are unafraid to ask for help. You must be willing to reach out to others to assist you on your journey. You for example have to set your own alarms at night. You have to decide you want to wake up early enough to go to the gym. But the part where self ends and someone else comes into the picture often is blurred and the distinction requires finesse, confidence and humility by being humble enough to ask for help. No one succeeds alone. Not even leaders. But more importantly, especially leaders. You can enlist the assistance of someone willing to help and remind you, by calling you when they wake up in the morning, but that requires asking. Maybe you decide to enlist the help of a gym coach to help you lose weight or achieve a personal goal or toning up your abs that too requires asking. All those are examples of personal self-motivation.

Leaders remember the ALWAYS:

Always make eye contact

Always speak clearly; enunciate

Always project genuineness

Always speak truth

Always put forth best effort

Always project confidence

Always show your fierceness

Always stand firm; be concise, yet

Always remember to show compassion

Always show respect

Always treat people fairly

Always prepare yourself; proactive

Always have a plan

Always amaze in delivery

Always remember to smile

Always execute objectives

The BE Simplicities:

BE Punctual. If you are on time, you are late. So be there early, at least 30 minutes early.

BE Humble, because a little humility takes you a long way.

BE Attentive, Make eye contact.

BE Optimistic, You should see positivity, even in impossibilities.

BE Willing, Put forth effort.

BE fierce, bold and unafraid.

BE firm, know when to hold your ground.

BE confident, Poise and Steady.

BE assertive, do not be passive or aggressive.

BE fair, Impartial and equal to all, including yourself.

BE prepared, Do your homework.

BE proactive, Plan to not be reactive.

BE Knowledgeable, impress your people with your intellect and memory.

BE Grateful, praise and reward your people and don't be shy about it.

BE yourself, don't pretend to be what you are not. People love genuineness.

BE approachable, smile and disarm your audience with kindness.

Be honest, truth will always set you free.

BE Decisive, never hesitate to prosecute

Leaders Take Action!

Wake Up Early:

Look this is not rocket science. Leaders wake up early. Waking up early is part of what allows you to have a successful day. There is a saying out there that is said so often that it has become a cliché. EARLY BIRD GETS THE WORM! If you wake up early, you will be up and charged full of energy ready to kick the day's butt. Take no names and no prisoners. Get up early so you can be ready on time and arrive. And if you get there early, you will never be late. There is a running joke in the military that says that those who wake up early before the sun comes up usually gets more done by 10:00 AM than most people do working a 9 to 5. It is not necessarily TRUE, but the point is that when you set priorities and standards starting with your day EARLY, it helps you shape how much you accomplish towards your goal. That readiness mindset will bring you closer to your successful goal in life. The important part of making sure you are able to wake up early is ensuring that you go to bed early enough to get a good night's sleep. Body needs rest. Sometimes you have to forgo late nights hanging out with friends and partying in order to get a good night's sleep. An early day will allow for you to plan and tackle any agenda early on without feeling tired, sluggish and dragging your feet.

Groom Yourself:

After waking up early, take the time to groom yourself. Shower with soap, water and put on lotion afterwards and smells goods. Shave, brush your teeth, comb or brush your hair. Put on deodorant, cut your nails, or make sure your nails are clean. Take time to groom yourself well so that you are presentable to others. Make yourself look good in the mirror. Look at yourself and smile. Be attractive. Don't be afraid to make yourself look appealing. Love yourself. People are more willing to follow leaders who present themselves as clean cut and well groomed.

Dress Yourself:

Put on your best clothes. Do not be afraid to wear the best outfit you have to work. Do not be afraid to dress your best to start your day. You want to look your best at all time. First impressions are last and you never know when that first impression you make will leave a lasting impression on your environment. If you put on an outfit and you think that outfit looks good in the mirror than you should wear it. Do not hesitate and second guess yourself. You are an amazing person. You look great. Believe in yourself. Do not look down on yourself. Don't judge yourself. Be confident in yourself. In that mirror, you should point and tell yourself that you look amazing and that your outfit looks amazing. And that it will impress everyone. Wear it with confidence.

In a setting where you full body is exposed the first thing that a person sees about you when they look at you are your shoes. So put on your best shoes. Shine them even. In the military we are told that your shoes or boots are the first things that people notice about you, so shine them. Make them glitter like gold, because most people will look down first and then up to look at your face. They will see two things - Your nicest pair of shoes and your well-groomed face and haircut, hairdo, lipstick – your visage speaks volumes.

Smell Good:

Do not be afraid to put on some nice cologne gentlemen. Ladies do not be afraid to put on some perfume or flower fragrance that makes you smell divine. People will not judge you for smelling good. They will compliment you. (They will however judge you if you smell like the opposite.) Point to that mirror and spray that smell good.

Tic Tac and or gum is always beneficial in situations where people are in close quarters. Do not hesitate to carry some in your pocket.

Good Body Posture:

Once you have showered, dressed and put on some smell good. You should stand up straight. Pride yourself in having good posture. Good posture equates to confidence and assertiveness. Stand tall and look into that mirror. Point with that knife hand and tell yourself that this is your day. Smile as you say to yourself that you are going to conquer everything in sight. All your goals in life are achievable. Success is there for the taking. Do not hesitate. Remember to be a leader. Listen more. And speak only to share good ideas and give good direction. **Stand tall, walk confidently, make eye contact and smile.**

Do not be afraid to smile, make eye contact, shake hands and look into the person's eyes as you shake hands. Pan the room and look around the environment and look into all eyes with enthusiasm, assertiveness and receptiveness. Eye contact shows respect and smiling shows empathy in positive situations.
Eye contact should be a quick catch and release, not prolong so as to not intimidate, challenge or make uncomfortable. Unless

you are specifically addressing the person at which point it is okay to prolong, look away momentarily to break and find your way back to continue speaking or finish the conversation strong.

Leaders Make Plans!

Make Plans:

Preparation plus opportunity equals success in all endeavors. Always know what you are getting into by having a good detail plan. Prepare yourself so that you are not reacting to every situation that you did not anticipate. If you are going on a road trip you do not just get in the car and go. You plan several days ahead about where it is you are going, what it is you are going to do there, what you will need and how much it will cost you? You find out what roads to take, where the gas stations are, what cities you will pass through, how many miles away it is and etc.?

The point is you don't just get up and go. Have a plan. Make due diligence about what you are trying to accomplish. Leaders do the same thing when they are leading and or have to accomplish certain goals. They don't simply come to a meeting and say this has to get done; clap and say now let's do it! And then turn around and leave. They prepare before that meeting. They come with plans and strategies about how to do it. Success in life is very much the same way. If you have a goal about something you want to achieve you have to plan out what the roadmap is going to look like. And execute. Make sure you know what it is that you want to achieve and find someone who has already achieved such things or have gone to such places? Because a lot of times they may have a roadmap already in place, you simply have to research it and follow it. There are many factors to consider and in the process of learning and researching about how to put together a plan you will discover many things, not just about yourself but also about what you are trying to achieve. A plan is a road map to a trip. You have to always have a good map to get to where you destination. Do not set on a path without having a plan A and a plan B to supplement in case things change don't go according to plan. In the military we use a term that says, that the only constant is change. That means that situations, environments and plans are always changing and therefore you have to be fluid and adaptive in your planning and goals. Preparation allows you to be ready. When plan A doesn't work, move to plan B in order to continue your objective. Always have a plan in place in case you have to adapt.

Short Term Plans:

Short term plans are plans that can be immediately executed as early as a few days away, a few weeks to a few months, even to a year out. Same as your long term plans. Write them down. These plans can be a bit more detail and inscriptive because they may delineate things that you need to accomplish immediately. And unlike long term plans, there may not be as many steps that are need to be taken in order to achieve them. Always focus on short term plans first and then move on to your long term plans.

Long Term Plans:

Plans that will take you anywhere from three to five years to achieve are known as long term plans. They can usually be something like finishing college, going to grad school or getting a certificate; a G.E.D. People make plans for getting married, having children or etc. Any plans for such long term initiatives can be as detailed as you need them to be or as vague as the achievement threshold allows. And there may be several steps that need to be taken in order to achieve long term plans, especially because they harder to reach. Many other short term achievements may need to happen. But the important thing to remember about making plans is that you should write them down. Put your plans on paper and put that paper somewhere that you can see it every day. Make a bulletin board, a dream sheet. Put it on the mirror that you look at yourself in everyday so that you are always reminded that your plans may not be immediate priority, they are still a priority in your life.

Plan of Actions and Milestones; POAM:

A plan is just a plan unless you take steps to move towards it. A POAM is an acronym used in the business world that describes a series of steps. It stands for: Plan of actions and milestones. It literally is a visual timeline of written steps delineating and describing specific goals and achievements that need to be done or deadlines to be met on your part in order to achieve your ultimate goal. The term POAM means that I have a plan and timeline that I am working on to reach an agenda. You have to physically make the process move, take the steps to push and manually walk it forward; otherwise it is just a plan on paper without any real progress. So set moves in motion by following your POAM and getting things done within a set timeline.

Know Your Environment:

Always pay attention to your surroundings. Have a map. Utilize all the resources at your disposal to maximize your awareness. Today in this day and age you probably have a smartphone with internet access on it. Use it to research information when you need. Use Google, yahoo, and any other web searching platform that is available to find answers that you are looking for. You can also find what you need by going to a Library. Be familiar with your city, your neighborhood; know where things are that can benefit you. Know your house, or apartment that you live in. Get to know the people around you and the individuals who your actions may influence consequently affect. Know you job environment or potential work environment. What is it that can further you along in that area and place? What can maximize your leadership potentials in that area of your expertise?

Being a subject matter expert is usually beneficial to you when you know and understand your environment and how your knowledge can increase your effectiveness as a leader.

Ask Questions:

Listen More! Always pay attention for clues. Remember being a good leader means that you are a great listener. It means also you are a good follower. In as much as other people are looking to you for clues and for leadership, you should be just as willing to follow by checking for clues as well. When you don't understand something, do not hesitate to ask questions. Don't pretend to know or understand something if you don't. Ask for clarification if you don't understand. Pretending to know something you really don't understanding is worse than being ignorant. It's foolish, hubris and can be more harmful to your reputation and expertise, even worse to the trust that people put in you as a leader. It is sometimes easier to admit that you do not know something and humbling yourself enough to learn than pretending you know and foolishly faltering when you are challenged with the truth.

Listen to People:

Listen more. Be attentive. Pay attention. Listen to what people are saying to you. Remember cues are subtle and not always expletive. Face your speaker, adjust your body towards the person who is speaking to you. Don't fiddle with your phone or be distracted by other things. Look at the person in their eyes and pay attention to their cues and gestures. Smile and don't frown. Be sincere and receptive. Listening to people is a good indication that you are comfortable, you are safe and you are at ease enough to be receptive. In turn that will make them feel comfortable. It will make the person speaking to you reciprocate your behavior. They will be less guarded and less apt to filter your ideas. They will feel safe; will be more open to receiving direction, advice and more willing to share ideas with you because they will see that you care.

Respond Politely:

There is nothing more beautiful when people walk away from one another smiling and at ease. It shows the absolutely graceful act of good leadership in motion. When another person walks up to you, ask you a question you have the opportunity to leave them wishing they didn't have to leave your presence, because you were so pleasant and kind. All because your response was kind. Your smile, your words politely telling them what they need to hear to help them about their day. There is never a need to be rude or ugly to anyone that trusts you enough to approach you in confidence and allowing you to lead them. Remember that leaders do not have time for misdirection and or misinformation. It doesn't take much to lose people's attention or trust. The easiest way to get people to stop trusting you is to respond to them impolitely, dismissively or with misinformation that leads them to the wrong path, or worse endangers their safety. The fastest way to get people to stop listening to you is to give them misinformation as a leader. You don't ever want to get to a point where people stop allowing you to lead them, because then what you become is no longer a leader, but simply an authority figure, otherwise known as a dictator; someone who makes people do, yet get nothing accomplished. Never be dismissive. Always be polite. Be reception, compassionate, be nice and be fair. Be firm, be truthful, be honest and people will always respect you for it.

Speak Clearly:

In whatever language you speak to people, always do so clearly. Always speak up for yourself. No need for mincing words or sugarcoating or sweet talking when you do not need to. Don't allow people to talk over you as you speak. And don't interrupt when you are spoken to. So that means you must speak up and speak clearly. Do so deliberately, intentionally without muddy or low monotone words that can sully or drown your meaning. Your intentions should always be spoken clearly, concisely with precision and pronunciation and dictation so that you do not confuse people. Speak so that they understand your meaning without ambiguity.

Don't use slang, unless it is part of the conversation or setting. Speak proper English or whichever language you choose to use in the moment that will be most receptive. And if you are not a subject matter expert, be mindful that language you use or borrow to make your point across is not seem as insulting or appropriating to the actual experts owners of the jargon you are using. Use technical language or on the job lingo only when it is appropriate and on the job only, not around people who would not understand it or a setting where it would confuse people.

Be direct, be subtle and be tactful – meaning do not be tacky and don't sound ridiculous. By repeating, tripping over words and speaking about things you do not understand or are not familiar with. And certainly don't make it up as you go. Make eye contact, smile and use subtle jokes only if and when appropriate and to the point.

Stand up straight. Don't cross your arms. Body posture is good when your arms are by your side and or you use one hand at a time by your waist to speak or motion politely. Do not point menacingly at people or flail around. It can give the wrong intentions.

Positive Optimism:

Strive to employ optimism in your life. Always remember to keep a positive attitude. A positive attitude will get you a lot farther in life than a negative, condescending or sarcastic attitude. A positive attitude tells the world that you are confident, assertive and optimistic. Optimism allows you to see the great potential in situations versus always seeing the negative and downside of a tasking or challenge. There is nothing wrong with looking in the mirror and saying positive and optimistic things about you.

I am a leader.

I am a thinker.

I am a problem solver.

I am confident.

I am strong.

I am able to complete any task.

I can do this.

I will do this.

I have no doubts about my abilities.

I have every confidence in myself and those around me.

I am optimistic about life. About living and about achieving.

Follow your Values:

Your values and morals make you who you are. Don't compromise yourself or beliefs.

Your values are what have been taught to you during your upbringing about right and wrong. That voice inside your mind which many people call a conscious. It tells you when things are wrong or right. It is a feeling of knowing when you are doing something that will help people, and make you feel good. It is also a feeling of knowing when you are hurting people and you don't feel good inside about those things. Without going into detail, your values are based on what you have learned in life and what you are accustomed to base on religion, culture and or political association. Good values always resonate with your conscious. It tells you when something is right and when it is wrong. Values are sometimes difficult to place depending on how you were raised. But you should always understand and keep in mind that how you treat people is how you should want them to treat you. If you want people to love you, to accept you, to praise you and to acknowledge your positive acts, then you should strive to do the same things for people you interact with as well. Do unto others what you want done unto you.

Self-Control:

We are reminded that as much as we have dreams, we have incredible drive and we have unlimited potential to become the best of ourselves, we also have personal hurdles. Those hurdles sometimes render us victims of our appetites. Appetites which in the moment can be interpreted as basic necessities. In hindsight those basic necessities in an improper environment can represent lack of self-control. Both pain and pleasure in the guise of comfort and hardship. As individuals these are not unique to our situations, nor to us alone. These appetites are shared with all society. Pain in the form of hunger, thirst and need of shelter. Pleasure in the form of sex, companionship, love, comfort, safety and need of sleep. These appetites can sometimes convince us that they are priority in the moment and therefore disregarding responsibility and care of a professional environment is okay. An undisciplined leader will think dismissing responsibility to himself, to his subordinates is convenient and forgivable, all the while not seeing the fallout. A discipline leader challenges impulses that are reckless and unproductive. He or she wields the moment in spite of basic appetites. Facing yourself in the moment and addressing the momentary incoherence and misjudgment can be quite beneficial in the long run. Self-control can save you much heartache if you choose to exercise it.

Leaders Execute Plans:

Always Follow Through:

Your plans and your goals are only that; plans and goals. It is absolutely up to you to make them happen. No one in life will give you anything for free. You have to earn every nickel and dime that you make. You have to work for every inch of success that you achieve. For every mile you walk, your feet and yours only will bear the pain and ache. Remember that! The saying that says walk a mile in my shoes is use often but is seldom understood because no one ever walks in other people's shoes. As a leader you simply have to remember that you aren't the only person with a goal in life. Others have goals too and are also searching for success. The success that you reach in life will also help and motivate others around you. It will make you a leader whether you want to be one or not. People will expect you to follow through and continue that path even when you think you have reached your pinnacle. Exercise and execute your plans and goals in every aspect of your life.

The Legendary knife hand is a tool. That is all it is. It is a subliminal tool used for pointing to a specific direction. Use it to point at a target of intention with plans of execution. You should use it daily to point at the mirror and to say self I am a leader and I need to act like it. I need to execute these plans that I have written down for my future. There is no question that leadership is not simply leading others. It is about leading yourself in the manner that will allow others to follow you. The legendary knife hand is effective as it is poignant. It has been used by countless leaders to delineate effective advice over years to very well deserving individuals as you on how to keep your minds sharp and leadership abilities keen. Some of these same advices helped me to change my life in many positive ways. As a Veteran, these same ideas allowed me to grow into the leader I became in the military. Some of my proudest moments as a leader were when I impacted people unknowingly. Those individuals sought me out later to tell me of instances that I helped to shape their goals for the better. The moments that I did not know I had impacted people I worked with, fueled my passion and made me want to go even farther in helping to mold others. They would come back to me and made sure that I knew I had made a difference in their lives and that was all the reward I needed. That is when I understood that I was accomplishing something meaningful for the people who called me leader. I never emphasized that I was a leader, I always knew it and they knew it because the relationship fostered presented itself as such, in reciprocal terms made to benefit, because we all listened. We listened and we all understood. And because they felt so inclined, my ideas were listened to. That reciprocity in term made us all successful. They listened to my ideas, they allowed me to lead them and I in term listened to them and built them up as leaders also.

The idea of leading oneself is not rocket science, so I will not try to present any more complicated material. The point of this entire manuscript is to just be you. Be truthful. Be receptive, be faithful enough in practicing those simple behaviors and they can allow you to grow, to reach a level of success in your life. You are the driver in the seat of the car. It is absolutely okay to drive yourself safely on the road. You can do that by ensuring that you have a map and a plan to get where you are going.

Leaders remember the ALWAYS:

Always make eye contact

Always speak clearly; enunciate

Always project genuineness

Always speak truth

Always put forth best effort

Always project confidence

Always show your fierceness

Always stand firm; be concise, yet

Always remember to show compassion

Always show respect

Always treat people fairly

Always prepare yourself; proactive

Always have a plan

Always amaze in delivery

Always remember to smile

Always execute objectives

The BE Simplicities:

BE Punctual, if you are on time, you are late. So be early. At least 30 minutes early.

BE Humble, a little humility takes you a long way.

BE Attentive, Make eye contact.

BE Optimistic, You should see positivity, even in impossibilities.

BE Willing, Put forth effort.

BE fierce, bold and unafraid.

BE firm, know when to hold your ground.

BE confident, Poise and Steady.

BE assertive, do not be passive or aggressive.

BE fair, Impartial and equal to all, including yourself.

BE prepared, Do your homework.

BE proactive, Plan to not be reactive.

BE Knowledgeable, Impress your people with your talent.

BE Grateful, praise and reward your people and don't be shy about it.

BE yourself, don't pretend to be what you are not. People love genuineness.

BE approachable, smile and disarm your audience with kindness.

Be honest, truth will always set you free.

BE Decisive, never hesitate to prosecute.

Simplicity vs Complexity:

Plan and execute with simplicity. Keep everything about your execution simple. Simplicity is a tool that people seldom use. The reason people have become unaccustomed to simplicity is because our lives are so embroiled in complication in this day and age that we forget that sometimes simplicity is the best way to go about solving problems. Keep things simple when it comes to dealing with life and dealing with some of the obstacles you encounter. Yes life can be complicated, but a leader is supposed to find ways to make plans and taskers simpler for the people who choose to work with them. Your plans and your goals will be as complicated as you decide to make them. Your mind has a tool bag full of useful ideas and sometimes, just maybe sometimes simplicity is one of the tools that may well do to solve some of the issues. Remember to keep it simple.

Complexity is the unforeseen, it is mathematics showing up in the middle of a spelling bee. Complexities can challenge our leadership in a way that sometimes reaffirm our strengths.

Unexpectedness can sometimes reveal a leader's incredible ability to be successful by persevering through unscathed or it could expose her or his weakness in a time that may be compromising and may prove most inconvenient. Leaders either overcome complexities or they are swept aside by them. Those trials come in many shapes, forms, sizes and circumstances. Everything that you have learn and have done before ever encountering adversity as a leader prepares you for the complexities that are sure to come. These complexities are all the things you don't want to see on your leadership path and I mean, it is everything that you did not plan for and shows up on the road anyway. Everything that was not discussed at the meetings you attended and was not put on paper and wasn't planned, but comes crashing down on the parade without invitation is what complexity is. It's called mathematics. Statistics and it comes around when one least expects. And sometimes even in quantities. As a leader complexity is expected. Complexity is what sets great leaders apart from mediocre ones. In a situation when things happen unexpectedly good leaders will utilize good judgement and sensible methods to contain and prosecute, subordinate situations that would otherwise completely deter goals. In any given time and place when a leader does not have the discipline and mental dexterity to properly curate complexities, he or she can become distracted and ruffled to the point of making mistakes. This is when a leader becomes reactive, and attempts to respond to unplanned circumstances in the worst way they know how – by reacting physically, emotionally. Discipline leaders react mentally, strategically, calmly and with poise because they understand that situations come unexpectedly. As a matter of fact, complexity was to be expected and that they have to be ready to wrestle with it head on. A leaders has absolutely no choice but to overcome the complexity, no matter how unpredictable. Leaders learn to master the art of dealing with the unexpected by planning and having secondary and even tertiary plans just in case the first plan doesn't work. That's why I say always have a plan A, and a plan B. And just in case, have a plan C. Leaders make plans and 100% of the time, a good leader will have 99.999999 percent confidence that the plans will work. A trained military special operations sniper will tell you, no two shots are ever the same. Reason being is that targets move, temperature fluctuates, time changes, plus factor in elevation, mood, fatigue, dexterity, experience and the list goes on forever. All you have is best practice. Unless a robot is executing your plans, you always have to be ready for change. In the military we are taught that the only constant is change. So you must always be prepared for complexity. Leaders plan because no matter how certain a circumstance is, the probability of something going wrong or not according to plan is still there. So be prepared just in case. Good leaders prepare by being disciplined, by being mentally sharp, being prepared, by being intuitive, by being astute, by being perceptive and by constantly learning and honing their leadership skill. A leader is a student of his or her craft. A leader is a lifelong learner and will always take the time to educate themselves, will study the details, the subtleties, always takes the time to learn about all the possibilities and complexities that may hinder goal completions. Complexities can be something as simple as tardiness because of traffic on the road, to very real world problems such as death in the family and loves ones in the hospital. Ironically in life and reality there are more complexities to be listed on charts, graphs and reasons for failures than there are simplicities to be listed on charts for successes.

A leader is intuitive by choice, not by nature because leadership intuition is honed not gifted, is cultivated not assumed. Intuition is a tool that is an integral part of the characteristics required for good leadership. It is an effectively essential part of a leader's tool bag. The ability to understand something immediately, by recognizing it without the need for conscious reasoning is crucial for good decision making. No intuition doesn't mean blind knowledge. It means common understanding of something that is known to occur or can reasonably occur based on experience, statistical practicality and understanding of schedule, statistics or planning otherwise unplanned. Intuition is something that comes from being disciplined mentally through practice, training and routine.

Complexities are just as the word infers – complex. They can be seemingly simple nuisances like; errors, dissent, tardiness, absences, illness, ignorance, disobedience, accidents to downright absurdities like misogyny, unexpected deaths, equal opportunity concerns, racism, xenophobia, threats, assaults and the listing goes on literally for miles, because there is no way all the things that can possibly go wrong in life can be accurately labeled here. This short book is not written to help you address all the problems of life. This short passage about complexity is merely a warning about leadership, ascribing the fact, that being a leader is not always so simple. Leadership is not merely the fun and authoritative aspects of possessing a title, but that leadership is supposed to challenge you. The requirements of Leadership beckons you to be prepared, challenges and fashions you in a way that will enable you to deal with very real and unexpected hardships that can test your abilities in life. And that you should be prepared. Good leaders are intuitive, they know to expect the unexpected. That is why as a leader you are a lifelong learner and lifelong follower, constantly honing your skills in order to stay at the forefront of expectations. Being in the fray sharpens your mind at which further sharpens your response. Your reaction is what can blunt and mitigate unexpected actions, so that you are not always reacting, but are prepared for every case that precipitates.

Strive for Balance:

Be balanced both mentally and physically. The greatest personal achievement that you can attain is leadership of yourself. That is the power of self-leadership, the power of self-control. The power to direct yourself into the path that will keep you grounded, that will allow you to be successful in every endeavor. I said at the beginning of this pamphlet that leadership is simply you and your ideas and it is true. Leadership is others allowing you to lead them because they trust you. That means they trust you and your ideas and that is what leadership is truly about. It is about you and how far you want to reach in life, how far you are willing to lead others. Leaders present their ideas to people in the world who are willing to listen. They present their incredible passions and thoughts to people who believe in them. People believe in the ideas of those leaders because they exude confidence and willingness to follow-through. And people will always believe in those kinds of leaders. Leaders present concepts to individuals who listen and follow, because they understand that these leaders have balance. They believe they know the way, they believe they have good clear heads and sound minds. Those listening therefore are receptive and are willing to help leaders build their dreams in exchange for some of that balance and peace of mind. Stable leadership is the most desirable human resource trait in modern civilization. That is why we have so many democratic elections in America and around the world. We are all looking for balance and stability.

I mentioned to you that there are good leaders and bad leaders out in the world. I told you that there are two things that you must understand about being a good leader. The first and most important thing about being a good leader is that leaders are always willing to listen. What I meant by that is that good leaders are always willing to put people first. They are not above and aren't so high and mighty to not consider people. Good principled leaders are followers first. The good leader that you are and have been has been listening to people for a very long time. At the same instance an ever better leader is someone who listens to the person in the mirror. You have good ideas too. You have good intentions and you have to always be willing to do the important things required of you in order to be successful. You have to follow, meaning you have to follow your dreams and the goals that you set for yourself and you have to be a leader for you. You must be the face in the mirror rooting for yourself and telling yourself that you have what it takes to be an amazing leader. You have what it takes to be successful.

The challenge will always be finding the proper balance between inner direction and outer influence. Balance is you listening to those you are leading outside the mirror and embracing the person within the mirror. Balance and stability of good leadership comes from articulating and interpreting confidence, drive, empathy and motivation that is appropriate, measurable enough to lead yourself and others without upsetting the balance. There are plenty of motivational books, videos and movies in the world to get you started. This pamphlet is not a detailed idea filled driver of what you need to do. It is simply a talking point for you when you stand in front of your mirror at home. It is a simple reminder to be vocal. It's a reminder to speak to you, for you. It is a reminder to stand your ground, to speak often to that person in the mirror, to compliment them, to reassure them, to motivate them. To use the metaphorical knife hand and point at yourself and say self, today you are a leader. Tomorrow you are a leader. Yesterday you were a leader and that as long as people will need direction and as long as you are in the driver's seat you will always be a leader to direct and point not only people towards good directions, but to point yourself in the right path.

Be always vocal in expressing your ideas. Do not hide from yourself. Do not hide from the face in the mirror. Remember that the hardest part of this is allowing you, the person in the mirror to accomplish the task of being a leader. You would do well to realize that you may be your staunchest adversary, but you can rest assure to know that you can overcome any obstacle when you put your knife hand forward and charge the obstacle. You and only you can convince yourself that you have what it takes to lead yourself out and through any situation that you encounter as counter-productive in this life. Remember you represent you in all aspects of what must be accomplished to reach any and all goals set before yourself. You are the face of your leadership. You are the face of leadership in the mirror. Remember to be humble. Listen More.

Confidence:

A leader with a good plan and a good idea is only able to execute those ideas if those around you feel comfortable and at ease around you. As a leader the most important part of leading is allowing those around you to be comfortable enough to listen to ideas you have to share. That happens notably when they are comfortable in your confidence. When they are at ease knowing that you have the knowledge, the know-how and their good interest at heart. You have to be sure of yourself.

Not cocky, bullish, or aggressive, but assertive, confident and sure of yourself. You have to make them feel safe. There is a difference between being a shy person who knows what your craft is and understands the properties of your ideas and how they work versus someone who is cocky and has no clue how to do the job. People will always know the difference. If you have an absolute understanding and are knowledgeable about what you are talking about, people will always want to listen because you are sure enough in yourself and it shows immediately when they look at you and when you speak about it.

The confidence of your idea projects itself even without them having knowledge of it. People have what are call truth detectors and will smell your confidence or lack of a mile away. Have you ever sat in a briefing and or a presentation, where the presenter was nervous, afraid, uneasy and uncomfortable? The audience immediately can smell that fear and they will mirror immediately what the person onstage is projecting. Once you make people feel uncomfortable and unsafe and they are no longer at ease, they will no longer be open to listen to your idea. There is nothing more that people hate than feeling uncomfortable. That is why we don't like public displays of affection, because if makes people uncomfortable. We also don't like public displays of violence, loudness, rudeness, sorrowful crying or kissing in public because it makes people fearful or uncomfortable. All of those display fear or uncertainty and exposes a person's inner doubts. People don't like fear. Fear is the opposite of confidence. Uncomfortable is the opposite of comfortable. And both of those are the opposite of confidence.

Confidence means it is okay to be at ease and comfortable around you. Be assertive and confident by knowing what you are talking about. Understand what it is you are sharing with people. You have to believe in it, otherwise they will not. That is why you must believe in yourself. Leadership starts with you, the person in the mirror and therefore your confidence comes from you being comfortable enough to stand in the mirror and convince you that you are a leader. You are your biggest fanatic; you and only you can explain your thoughts. Be the subject matter of yourself and your ideas.

Lifelong Long Leadership:

There is not a day when you will wake up, where you will be able to look in the mirror and say that you are not a leader. Your attitude and habits may change overtime. Your leadership style may change and take on new roles, but your leadership face cannot be hidden, no matter how many masks you may put on. You are a leader now. You have been a leader all your life. You will continue to be a leader for as long as others will acknowledge that you have good enough ideas to share and pass on. As long as people can continue to feel safe and comfortable around you to hear what you have to communicate to them you will always be a leader. The thing about being a leader is that we change and adapt base on our environment and the people around us. We learn, we absorb, and we see and build our leadership style to help make us better people and make the people around us better as well. Leaders are not selfish. We are selfless. We go out of our way to help people. Leaders go off the beaten path, out of our way to help people see things in themselves that have always been there. We help clear the brush and make way for future leaders. We help them to find their strengths and to project their ideas. We also help them to share those ideas with others. That is what leaders do. Leaders change their world with their selfless devotion to others. Leaders are not great because they do great things, they are ordinary people who wake up early in the mornings every day, who dress themselves, and go out in the world and share their thoughts and do it well enough that others tell of their shared deeds. Their selfless acts are told and shared enough times that they are considered great overtime. A leader is someone who is a lifelong sharer of knowledge. Because leaders are always learning and are constantly evolving, they are always shaping and grooming themselves, always sharpening their minds and in doing so will always find reason to continue sharing, helping and shaping society. People will always be willing to listen to them because they are never short of good ideas. Presidents, Generals, Admirals, Diplomats and CEO's of great Companies are always being sought after for their knowledge even after they retire because they know those people are never short of good ideas. Lifelong leadership is a trait that comes with being a leader. The face of leadership cannot and will not shy away from you even when you put away the mirror. You should embrace the leader in the mirror and start honing and shaping your personal skills to make people comfortable and accepting around you. In so that one day people will trust you enough to listen to your ideas. Remember the knife hand points at you and tells you that you are the greatest reason for being successful. You can break or build your chances of success. You can build it, you can feed it and you can fuel it until it catches fire. In the end your ideas can fuel and propel you to the highest state of selflessness. The state of selflessness is simply the place where people look at you and see a great leader.

The End

The best short book today on leadership. A self-reflection of the person in the mirror. A simple guide on how to envision yourself as the kind of leader others will be willing to follow by being brilliant on the simplicities of self-leadership.

www.ingramcontent.com/pod-product-compliance
Lightning Source LLC
Chambersburg PA
CBHW071423210526
45465CB00001B/499